DISASTER ZONE
DROUGHTS

by Cari Meister

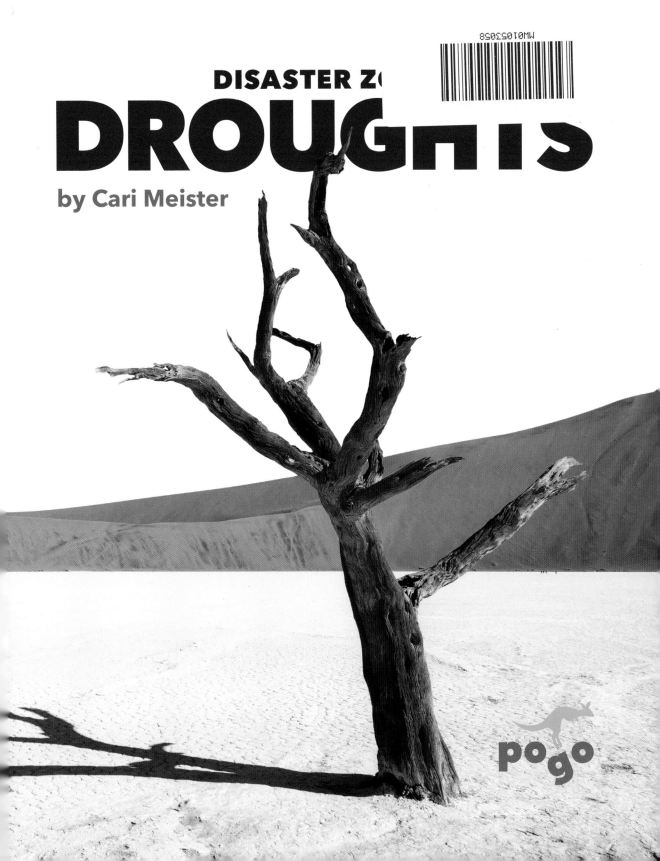

Ideas for Parents and Teachers

Pogo Books let children practice reading informational text while introducing them to nonfiction features such as headings, labels, sidebars, maps, and diagrams, as well as a table of contents, glossary, and index.

Carefully leveled text with a strong photo match offers early fluent readers the support they need to succeed.

Before Reading

- "Walk" through the book and point out the various nonfiction features. Ask the student what purpose each feature serves.
- Look at the glossary together. Read and discuss the words.

Read the Book

- Have the child read the book independently.
- Invite him or her to list questions that arise from reading.

After Reading

- Discuss the child's questions. Talk about how he or she might find answers to those questions.
- Prompt the child to think more. Ask: Have you ever experienced a drought? What can you do to conserve water?

Pogo Books are published by Jump!
5357 Penn Avenue South
Minneapolis, MN 55419
www.jumplibrary.com

Library of Congress Cataloging-in-Publication Data

Meister, Cari, author.
  Droughts / by Cari Meister.
      pages cm. – (Disaster zone)
  "Pogo Books are published by Jump!."
  Audience: Ages 7-10
  Includes index.
  ISBN 978-1-62031-224-7 (hardcover: alk. paper) –
  ISBN 978-1-62031-264-3 (paperback) –
  ISBN 978-1-62496-311-7 (ebook)
  1. Droughts–Juvenile literature. I. Title.
  QC929.25.M45 2016
  551.57'73–dc23

                                              2014048960

Series Editor: Jenny Fretland VanVoorst
Series Designer: Anna Peterson
Photo Researcher: Anna Peterson

Photo Credits: All photos by Shutterstock except: Alamy, 16; Corbis, 5; Dreamstime, 4; Getty, 17; iStock, 18-19; National Geographic, 13; Thinkstock, 12, 14-15.

Printed in the United States of America at Corporate Graphics in North Mankato, Minnesota.

TABLE OF CONTENTS

CHAPTER 1

WHAT IS A DROUGHT?

Imagine you are in Australia. The ground is cracked. Plants are dead. Dust blows in the air.

Some people wear masks. It keeps the dust out of their lungs. There are tanks around houses to collect rainwater. But there's no water in them. It's a drought!

A drought happens when there is too little rain for too long a time. Plants die. Rivers and lakes dry up. Sometimes the ground gets very hard. It cracks open.

DID YOU KNOW?

Australia's Millennium Drought was one of the worst in history for the southeast part of the country. It lasted from 1997 to 2009. That's 12 years!

Droughts can cause **famines**, floods, and fires. A famine happens when people can't grow enough food. People starve to death.

Droughts can cause floods. When a dry area finally gets rain, the ground is hard. The rain does not soak in.

Wildfires happen during droughts. Dead trees catch fire. If it is windy, the fire spreads fast.

DID YOU KNOW?

Helicopters fly in to help stop wildfires. They have special tanks that release water over fires.

CHAPTER 2

WHERE AND WHEN?

Droughts are hard to **predict**.

Hydrologists study past and present droughts. What they learn helps them predict when and where a new drought will happen.

Droughts happen all over the world. But places with a warm **climate**, high winds, and low rainfall are more likely to experience drought.

WHERE DO THEY HAPPEN?

Most of the areas where drought is common are in the **Southern Hemisphere**.

■ = Drought Zones

CHAPTER 3

DEADLY DROUGHTS

Between 1934 and 1937 there was a drought in the **Great Plains**. It was known as the **Dust Bowl**. The wind picked up the dirt from the fields and carried it high into the air.

Large clouds of dirt blew through the country. They **suffocated** animals and made it hard for people to breathe.

Ethiopia has a history of drought. For much of the 1980s, it did not rain. Crops dried up. Animals and people did not get enough food. About a million people starved to death.

DID YOU KNOW?

The Dust Bowl taught farmers that they had not been using the land correctly. Today farmers give the soil time to rest between plantings.

It is up to us to take care of our water supply.

Turn off the faucet when you brush your teeth.

Take short showers.

Use a bucket and sponge to wash a car, not a hose.

Do not water your lawn.

How else can you help **conserve** water?

ACTIVITIES & TOOLS

HOW DROUGHT AFFECTS THE SOIL

This activity shows the effect of drought on the soil. By not watering one of the pots and then putting water in it after three weeks, you can see how the soil reacts to rain after it has been dry for a long time.

What You Need:

- soil
- two pots
- water

❶ Fill each pot with soil.

❷ Place the pots in a sunny place.

❸ Label one A. Label the other pot B.

❹ Water the soil in pot A every other day. Do not water pot B.

❺ After three weeks, water the soil in pot B.

❻ What happens to water in pot B? Is it absorbed into the dirt?

GLOSSARY

climate: The usual weather for a particular area.

conserve: To preserve and avoid wasteful use.

Dust Bowl: A period in the 1930s during which the Great Plains suffered from severe dust storms.

Ethiopia: A country in eastern Africa.

famine: When a large group of people do not have enough to eat.

Great Plains: The area of flat prairie land that lies between the Rocky Mountains and the Mississippi River.

hydrologists: Scientists that study Earth's water supply.

predict: To say that something might happen in the future.

Southern Hemisphere: The half of the world that lies below the equator.

suffocate: When animals or people die because they cannot breathe.

INDEX

TO LEARN MORE

Learning more is as easy as 1, 2, 3.

1) Go to www.factsurfer.com

2) Enter "droughts" into the search box.

3) Click the "Surf" to see a list of websites.

With factsurfer, finding more information is just a click away.